Van Stelle

SUNDAY

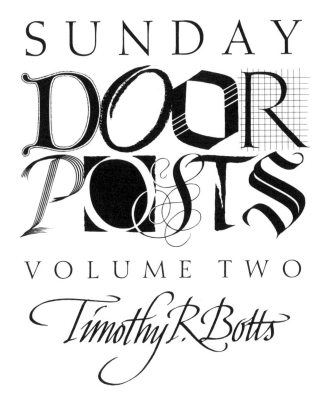

DOOR POSTS

VOLUME TWO

Timothy R. Botts

SHEED & WARD

The Title *Sunday Doorposts* is adapted from *Doorposts,* also by Timothy R. Botts, published by Tyndale House Publishers.

Scripture taken from the New American Standard Bible, ©1960, 1962, 1963, 1968, 1971, 1972, 1973, 1975, 1977 by The Lockman Foundation. Used by permission.

Scripture quotations marked (NIV) are from the Holy Bible, New International Version. Copyright© 1973, 1978, 1984 International Bible Society. Used by permission of Zondervan Bible Publishers.

Verses marked TLB are taken from *The Living Bible*© 1971. Used by permission of Tyndale House Publishers, Wheaton, IL. All rights reserved.

Verses marked TEV are from *Good News Bible* (Today's English Version) © American Bible Society. Used by permission.

Sheed & Ward™ is a service of National Catholic Reporter Publishing Company, Inc.

ISBN: 1-55612-462-7

Published by: Sheed & Ward
115 E. Armour Blvd. P.O. Box 419492
Kansas City, MO 64141

To order, call: (800) 333-7373

LET'S NOT
HAVE ANY
QUARRELING
BETWEEN
YOU AND ME...
FOR WE ARE
BROTHERS

from GENESIS 13:8 NIV

GOD laughter
has brought laughter laughter
me laughter laughter
laughter laughter
laughter laughter
laughter laughter
laughter laughter
laughter laughter
laughter laughter
laughter laughter
laughter laughter
laughter laughter laughter
laughter laughter
laughter laughter
laughter laughter
laughter laughter laughter
laughter laughter laughter
laughter laughter
laughter laughter
laughter laughter
laughter laughter
laughter

from GENESIS 21:6 NIV

WHAT HE DID WAS DISPLEASING IN THE SIGHT OF THE LORD

FROM GENESIS 38:10 NAS

YOU WILL SURELY
YOU WEAR OUT
WEAR WILL
YOU OUT SURELY
YOU WILL SURELY
FOR WEAR OUT
WILL SURELY
FOR WILL OUT
SURELY
THE TASK
IS TOO
HEAVY FOR YOU
YOU CANNOT
DO IT

from Exodus 18:18 NAS

ALONE

YOU SHALL HAVE NO
OTHER GODS BEFORE ME
YOU SHALL NOT MAKE FOR
YOURSELF AN IDOL
YOU SHALL NOT TAKE
THE NAME OF THE LORD
YOUR GOD IN VAIN
REMEMBER THE SABBATH DAY
TO KEEP IT HOLY
HONOR YOUR FATHER
AND YOUR MOTHER
YOU SHALL NOT MURDER
YOU SHALL NOT COMMIT ADULTERY
YOU SHALL NOT STEAL
YOU SHALL NOT BEAR
FALSE WITNESS AGAINST
YOUR NEIGHBOR
YOU SHALL NOT COVET

from EXODUS 20 NAS

WHEN
MY GLORY
PASSES BY,
I will put you
in a cleft
in the rock
and cover you
with my hand
until I have
passed by.

EXODUS 33 : 22 NIV

Have I not commanded you?
Be strong and
courageous,
Do not be terrified;
Do not be discouraged,
FOR
THE LORD
YOUR GOD
will be with you
WHEREVER YOU GO

JOSHUA 1:9
NIV

And David danced before the Lord with all his might.

I'm willing to act like a fool in order to show my joy in the Lord.

2 SAMUEL 6:14, 21 TLB

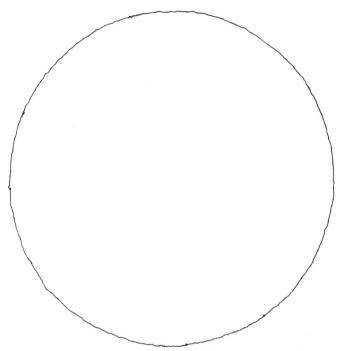

Because the Lord is my Shepherd, I have everything
I need! ◆He lets me rest in the meadow grass and leads me
beside the quiet streams. He gives me new strength. He helps
me do what honors him the most. ◆Even when walking through the
dark valley of death I will not be afraid, for you are close beside me,
guarding, guiding all the way. ◆You provide delicious food for me
in the presence of my enemies. you have welcomed me as your guest;
blessings overflow! ◆Your goodness and unfailing kindness shall
be with me all of my life, and afterwards I will live with you
forever in your home. ◆Psalm 23 TLB

Be of

WAIT

good courage

ON

and he will

THE

strengthen

LORD

your heart

FROM PSALM 27:14 KJV

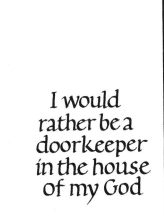

I would
rather be a
doorkeeper
in the house
of my God

than dwell
in the tents
of the wicked

from PSALM 84:10 NIV

TODAY
If you would
hear His voice
DO NOT
harden
your hearts.

from PSALM 95: 7, 8 NAS

TRUST IN THE LORD
with all your heart
and lean not on your own understanding
IN ALL YOUR WAYS
ACKNOWLEDGE HIM
and he will make your paths straight

PROVERBS 3:5-6 NIV

Do not despise
the Lord's discipline,
and do not resent
his rebuke,
because
the Lord disciplines
those he loves.

from PROVERBS 3:11,12 NIV

Rejoice in the wife of your youth. A loving doe, a graceful deer. May her breasts satisfy you always. May you ever be captivated by her love.

FROM PROVERBS 5:18-19 NIV

REVERENCE
FOR GOD
GIVES A MAN
DEEP STRENGTH

his children have a place of refuge and security

PROVERBS 14:26 TLB

THE
LORD
has
anointed
me to
bring
good
news
to the
suffering
and
afflicted.

from Isaiah 61:1 TLB

FOR I KNOW THE PLANS I HAVE FOR YOUR LIVES SAYS THE PLANS THEY ARE NOT FOR EVIL AND GIVE YOU A FUTURE TO AND A HOPE FOR GOOD

JEREMIAH 29:11

TLB

from Zechariah 4:6 NIV

NOT
BY
MIGHT
NOR
BY
POWER

but by my Spirit

SAYS THE LORD ALMIGHTY

Why do you look at the *speck* that is in your brother's eye, but do not notice the **LOG** that is in your own eye?

MATTHEW 7:3 NAS

Then
Jesus came
to them
and said,
ALL
AUTHORITY
IN HEAVEN
AND
ON EARTH
HAS BEEN
GIVEN
TO ME
Therefore
go
and
make
disciples
of all
nations

from Matthew 28:18,19
NIV

Do you have eyes but fail to see?

MARK 8:18 NIV

MARY SAID, I am the Lord's servant, and I am willing to do whatever he wants, from LUKE 1=38 TLB

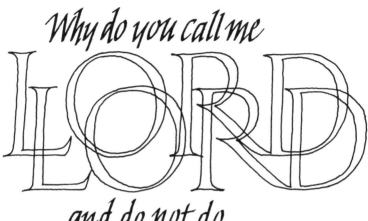

Why do you call me LORD and do not do what I say?

LUKE 6:46 NIV

But while he was still a long way off, his father saw him and was filled with compassion for him; he ran to his son, threw his arms around him and kissed him.

Father, I have sinned against heaven and against you. I am no longer worthy to be called your son.

from LUKE 15 : 18 & 20 NIV

JOHN 6:35 NIV

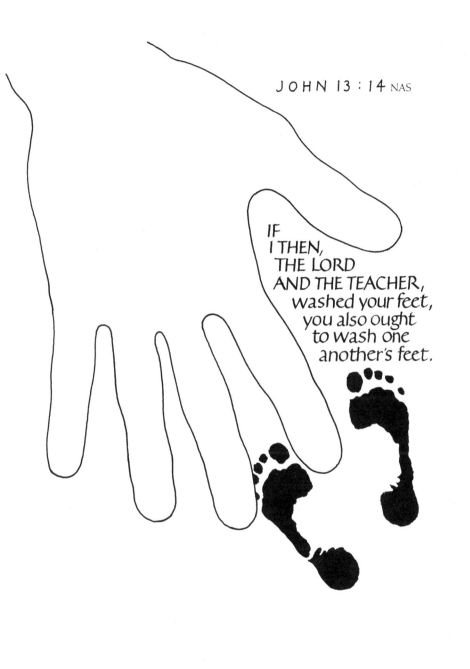

JOHN 13 : 14 NAS

IF
I THEN,
THE LORD
AND THE TEACHER,
washed your feet,
you also ought
to wash one
another's feet.

Let not your
heart be troubled;
believe in God,
believe also in Me.

JESUS

I am the way, and
the truth, and the
life; no one comes
to the Father,
but through Me.

In My Father's house are
many dwelling places;
if it were not so, I would
have told you; for I go
to prepare a place for you.

And if I go and
prepare a place
for you, I will
come again, and
receive you to My-
self; that where
I am, there you
may be also.

from JOHN 14 : 1 - 6 NAS

I tell you the truth,
anyone who has faith in me
will do what I have been doing.
He will do even greater things than these,
because I am going to the Father.

JOHN 14:12 NIV

COMFORTER
HELPER
ADVOCATE
COUNSELOR

I will
not leave
you as
orphans

FROM JOHN 14:18

NIV

I am the
Vine
you are the branches.
he who abides
in Me, and I in him
he bears much
fruit

For apart from Me
you can do nothing

JOHN 15 : 5 NAS

That they may all be one

from JOHN 17:21 NAS

SO RUN YOUR RACE TO WIN

1 CORINTHIANS 9:24 TLB

IN GOD'S PLAN
IN GOD'S PLAN
IN GOD'S PLAN
IN GOD'S PLAN
IN GOD'S PLAN
IN GOD'S PLAN
IN GOD'S PLAN
IN GOD'S PLAN
IN GOD'S PLAN
IN GOD'S PLAN

men &women need each other

from 1 Corinthians 11:11 TLB

LOVE
SO
bears all things
FAITH
believes all things
HOPE
hopes all things
LOVE
endures all things
A B I D E
these three but the
greatest
1 CORINTHIANS
13 : 7, 13
NAS
of these is
LOVE

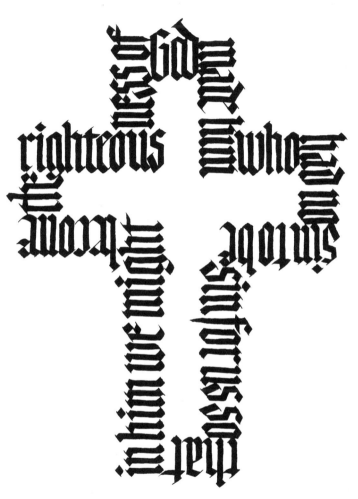

2 Corinthians 5:21
NIV

GOD sometimes uses sorrow in our lives to help us turn away from sin

from
2 CORINTHIANS
7:10 TLB

Thanks be to God for his indescribable gift!

2 CORINTHIANS 9:15
NAS

YOU · ARE · ALL · ONE · IN · UNION.

So there is no difference
between JEWS and
GENTILES
GALATIANS 3 : 28 TEV
between
SLAVES and free men
between men and Women

· WITH · CHRIST · JESUS ·

BUT WHEN THE GOD RIGHT TIME SENT FINALLY his CAME only Son

from GALATIANS 4:4 TEV

...that
you
may
know
him
better

from EPHESIANS 1:17 NIV

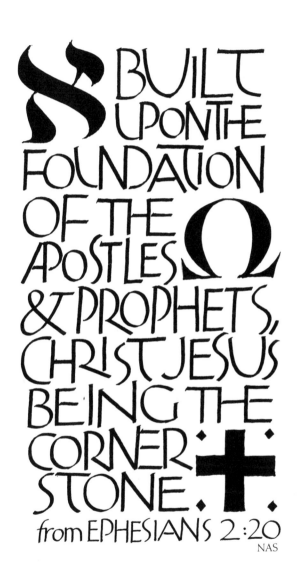

BUILT UPON THE FOUNDATION OF THE APOSTLES & PROPHETS, CHRIST JESUS BEING THE CORNERSTONE.

from EPHESIANS 2:20

NAS

FELLOW
HEIRS
FELLOW
MEMBERS
FELLOW
PARTAKERS

from EPHESIANS 3:6 NAS

Glory be to God
who by his mighty power
at work within us
is able to do
far more
than we would
ever dare to ask
or even dream of

from EPHESIANS 3:20 TLB

BE DILIGENT TO PRESERVE THE UNITY OF THE SPIRIT IN THE BOND OF PEACE

from EPHESIANS 4:3 NAS

BE ANGRY AND YET DO NOT SIN

DO NOT LET THE SUN GO DOWN ON YOUR ANGER

EPHESIANS 4:26 NAS

BE IMITATORS OF GOD
BE IMITATORS OF GOD

AS BELOVED CHILDREN
AS BELOVED CHILDREN

EPHESIANS 5:1 NAS

Do not get drunk with wine
which will only ruin you
instead
be filled
with the
Spirit

EPHESIANS 5 : 18 TEV

STRAINING TOWARD WHAT IS AHEAD

FORGETTING WHAT IS BEHIND

from PHILIPPIANS 3:13 NIV

Give thanks
in all
circumstances
for this is
God's will
for you in
Christ Jesus

1 THESSALONIANS 5:18 NIV

AND NOW flee from youthful lusts AND PURSUE RIGHTEOUSNESS FAITH LOVE AND

from
2 Timothy
2:22 NAS

we wait
for
the
blessed
hope,
the
glorious,
appearing
of
our
great
God
and
Savior
Jesus
Christ

FROM TITUS 2:13 NIV

*See to it that no one
misses the grace of God.*

FROM HEBREWS 12:15 NIV

In God's
great
mercy
he has given us
new birth
into a living hope
through
the resurrection
of Jesus Christ
from the dead.

from 1 PETER 1:3 NIV

THESE TRIALS ARE ONLY TO TEST YOUR FAITH TO SEE WHETHER OR NOT IT IS STRONG OR PURE IT IS BEING TESTED AS FIRE TESTS GOLD AND PURIFIES IT and your faith is far more precious to God than mere gold.

from 1 PETER 1:7 TLB

BE SHEPHERDS OF GOD'S FLOCK THAT IS UNDER YOUR CARE, SERVING AS OVERSEERS—NOT BECAUSE YOU MUST, BUT BECAUSE YOU ARE WILLING, AS GOD WANTS YOU TO BE; NOT GREEDY FOR MONEY, BUT EAGER TO SERVE

1 PETER 5:2 NIV

Do not love the world, nor the things in the world

FROM I JOHN 2:15 NAS

from REVELATION 2:17 NIV

TO HIM WHO OVERCOMES

I will give some of the hidden manna

I will also give him a white stone with a new name written on it, known only to him who receives it.

I AM HE
WHO SEARCHES
HEARTS AND MINDS
AND I WILL REPAY
EACH OF YOU
ACCORDING TO
YOUR DEEDS

from Revelation 2:23
NIV

I have
placed
before you
an open door
that
no one
can shut

from REVELATION 3:8 NIV

INDEX

Genesis 13:8, *Quarreling between brothers*
Genesis 21:6, *Laughter*
Genesis 38:10, *Displeasing in His sight*
Exodus 18:18, *The task is too heavy*
Exodus 20, *The ten commandments*
Exodus 33:22, *A cleft in the rock*
Joshua 1:9, *Be strong and courageous*
2 Samuel 6:14,21, *David danced*
Psalm 23, *The Lord is my Shepherd*
Psalm 27:14, *Be of good courage*
Psalm 84:10, *A doorkeeper*
Psalm 95:7-8, *Hear His voice*
Proverbs 3:5-6, *Trust in the Lord*
Proverbs 3:11-12, *The Lord's discipline*
Proverbs 5:18-19, *The wife of your youth*
Proverbs 14:26, *Deep strength*
Isaiah 61:1, *Good news to the suffering*
Jeremiah 29:11, *Plans for good*
Zechariah 4:6, *Not by might*
Matthew 7:3, *The log in your eye*
Matthew 28:18-19, *Go and make disciples*
Mark 8:18, *Do you have eyes?*
Luke 1:38, *I am the Lord's servant*
Luke 6:46, *Lord, Lord*
Luke 15:18,20, *Father, I have sinned*
John 6:35, *The bread of life*
John 13:14, *Wash one another's feet*
John 14:1-6, *I am the way*
John 14:12, *Even greater things*
John 14:18, *I will not leave you*

John 15:5, *I am the vine*
John 17:21, *All one*
1 Corinthians 9:24, *Race to win*
1 Corinthians 11:11, *Men and women*
1 Corinthians 13:7,13, *The greatest is love*
2 Corinthians 5:21, *The righteousness of God*
2 Corinthians 7:10, *Sorrow in our lives*
2 Corinthians 9:15, *His indescribable gift*
Galatians 3:28, *No difference*
Galatians 4:4, *The right time*
Ephesians 1:17, *That you may know*
Ephesians 2:20, *The cornerstone*
Ephesians 3:6, *Fellow heirs*
Ephesians 3:20, *Glory be to God*
Ephesians 4:3, *The bond of peace*
Ephesians 4:26, *Your anger*
Ephesians 5:1, *Imitators of God*
Ephesians 5:18, *Filled with the Spirit*
Philippians 3:13, *What is ahead*
1 Thessalonians 5:18, *In all circumstances*
2 Timothy 2:22, *Flee youthful lusts*
Titus 2:13, *The glorious appearing*
Hebrews 12:15, *The grace of God*
1 Peter 1:3, *In God's great mercy*
1 Peter 1:7, *Trials to test your faith*
1 Peter 5:2, *Shepherds of God's flock*
1 John 2:15, *Do not love the world*
Revelation 2:17, *To him who overcomes*
Revelation 2:23, *He who searches hearts*
Revelation 3:8, *An open door*